IMAGES
of England

WESTON-SUPER-MARE
1950s TO 1970s

Cover of the Town Guide, 1953.

IMAGES
of England

WESTON-SUPER-MARE
1950s TO 1970s

Compiled by
Sharon Poole

TEMPUS

First published 2001
Copyright © Sharon Poole, 2001

Tempus Publishing Limited
The Mill, Brimscombe Port,
Stroud, Gloucestershire, GL5 2QG

ISBN 0 7524 2173 5

Typesetting and origination by
Tempus Publishing Limited
Printed in Great Britain by
Midway Clark Printing, Wiltshire

High Street decorated for the coronation, 1953.

Contents

Acknowledgements

I am indebted to two local photographers for the majority of the pictures here. Edward Amesbury, for many years a staff photographer on the *Weston Mercury* newspaper, and keen spare-time photographer is the first. And secondly, Leslie Sandys, a professional photographer, who did a lot of work for the Borough Council Publicity Department, as well as local estate agents. Mr Sandys gave his entire collection of negatives – some 20,000 – to the Museum Service, and they form a unique and detailed record of the town from the 1950s when he moved to Weston, in the 1980s when he retired.

The remaining photographs come from two sources. In 1958, the Museum mounted an exhibition entitled *Life in our Town*. This consisted of over 200 photographs of everyday life in Weston-super-Mare taken by local amateur photographers. The images were donated to the Museum to create a lasting record of one year in the life of our town. The last source is photographs taken by myself. When the Museum moved to its new premises in Burlington Street in 1975, the local history collections were split between the Museum Service and the Library. One of the first tasks set by the new curator, Jane Evans, was to create a photographic record of the town. I spent many hours walking the streets and back alleys with a camera recording the kind of details so often lost without noticing such as enamel advertising signs, architectural details, date stones and old shop fronts.

Introduction

The period 1950–1970 may seem too recent to be the subject of a book of archive photographs. I'm sure to many people it seems like the blink of an eye since those days. However, in these thirty to fifty years, Weston-super-Mare, together with many other towns, has seen perhaps the biggest changes to its appearance since the mid-nineteenth century. This was the period when everyone went 'modern'; when technology became king, even if 1950s technology seems like the dark ages by today's standards! This period saw the rise of the teenager, the growth of American influences and music and the acceptance of the television into everyone's home. These factors saw ideas spread faster than ever before and it is perhaps the increasing speed of change that makes this period so different from those before.

In the 1950s wartime controls still operated, with the rationing of some items not lifted until 1953. The Festival of Britain opened in 1951 with the main exhibition in London. This was intended to lift people's spirits after the Second World War and to showcase new British products. As with the Millennium celebrations, all around the country small projects were implemented to tie in with the event. In Weston, the improvements to the Floral Clock were the most visible of these schemes.

Among the social changes was the growth of private car ownership. This had a far-reaching impact on the face of the town, as increasing space for car parking was required, both public and private. Bomb sites were used as temporary car parks and hedges, walls and lawns were removed from front gardens to become car standing spaces.

The 1960s also saw the final years of the Great British Seaside Holiday as it had been celebrated for over one hundred years. Foreign resorts became much more accessible as cheaper air travel became available. The lure of almost certain sun was too much for British resorts to compete with and it took many years for them to accept that changes had to take place if they wanted to survive.

In the 1960s and 1970s, much changed in Weston. It was the era of demolish rather than re-use. There was little sympathy for the architectural survivals of previous eras. In this period Weston lost the whole Carlton Street area along with many notable buildings – Villa Rosa, Etonhurst, Glentworth Hall, St John's School to name but a few. In fact, one of the few buildings to undergo conversion rather than demolition, was the Gaslight Company Workshops – converted to house Woodspring Museum (now the Time Machine museum) and opened in 1975. You could however, still walk along side alleys and back lanes and discover little forgotten corners of the town. What I did find, whilst trying today to place some of the buildings in the pictures, was how disorientating it can be. Some of the images have no present point of reference left. For example, in the photograph on p78 of the fire station in Beach Road, there are no surviving buildings from the photograph and it is very hard to picture it today.

So, what pictures have I chosen? Weston was still based around the holiday trade and the first chapter reflects this with pictures of hotels, beach scenes and leisure activities. I make no apology for including a lot of shops. Besides a personal fascination with old shops and their goods, it seems to me to be one of the areas that has seen the most change in this period. In the 1950s and even early 1960s, many shops still retained a Victorian feel about their fittings and window displays. There were still many small family-run specialist traders. In photographs of the mid-1960s you can see the change begin as new shopfronts were fitted, 'modern' displays mounted and new goods start to be stocked – especially electrical equipment. There are strange juxtapositions of 1960s plain glass windows next to detailed Victorian wooden frontages. Then gradually the modern style of one large pane of glass in a metal frame began to dominate the scene. Shops also began to be less specialist and to diversify their ranges. This period also saw the rise of totally new types of store – the supermarkets and DIY warehouses that dominate the retail trade today.

There is also a chapter on local industries. Some of these were barely changed from Victorian days, others were very new to the town. After the Second World War, the local authority actively promoted Weston as an ideal location for light industry. As tourism waned, so new jobs were needed and vacant wartime factories provided ideal premises. This leads nicely into a chapter entitled Our Changing Town. This features buildings and streets from all over the town and highlights the changes that have taken place over the thirty years.

Because the 1950s – 1970s was also the period when the boundaries between Weston and the surrounding villages began to blur, I have also included a few images of Worle, Uphill and Kewstoke. Worle, particularly, saw huge alterations to the face of the village, especially in the High Street. The population of Worle was predicted to rise to over 20,000 during this period and developments took place to cater for this increase, including new shops and a branch library.

I hope you will find the selection as interesting to look through as I have found it to compile. There is still much to be proud of in Weston and, as I always say, to plan for the future you need to have knowledge of the past, if only to avoid the same mistakes!

Sharon Poole
January 2001

One

A Town by the Sea

Bank Holiday crowds at Anchor Head, 5 August 1957. Anchor Head has always been a popular spot for sunbathing as it is a naturally sheltered bay. It was because of this that it was chosen as the Ladies Bathing Place in the earliest days of the resort. Note the two couples in the foreground, the girls sporting very fashionable handbags!

A general view of the Grand Pier and Knightstone from Worlebury Iron Age Hillfort, 1967. On Knightstone, the theatre (left) and swimming baths can be clearly seen. In the distance is Mendip.

The Grand Pier from the top of Weston Bus Station. The half-timbered building was the Tourist Information Bureau, built in the 1920s. This was replaced in 1973 by the present stone building (see p26).

Weston seafront at the entrance to the Grand Pier, 6 August 1964. Bank holiday crowds pack the promenade. In 1969, the old Edwardian entrance to the Grand Pier with its kiosks and cast iron turnstiles, was demolished and the present structure built, with arcades, souvenir and fish and chip shops.

The snack bar in the Oxford Street Shelter at 7.30 a.m., 13 April 1958. From left to right is J. Stacy, K. Tozer, Miss J. Giles, F. Crane, H. Snelgrove, Mrs F. Crane, S. Ford, W. Francis. Presumably these people are having breakfast before going to work.

The Beach Hotel, Royal Parade, 4 May 1959. These buildings were rather elegant in an elaborate mid-nineteenth century style. Today, there is a mixture of stalls selling seaside souvenirs and ice cream, adorning the frontage.

A wet Sunday afternoon, 24 August 1958. Visitors shelter by the entrance to the Grand Pier.

The rose walk at the Winter Gardens, photographed from the roof of the post office, 1974. This was a very popular place to sit in the summer, and deckchairs could be hired from the Winter Gardens. The Starlight Room, bar and tennis courts were demolished in 1990 and a new conference centre built as part of a complete redevelopment of the Winter Gardens.

Entrance to the Winter Gardens from Post Office Road, 24 September 1959. This gateway was broken up when the Town Square and Sovereign Centre were built. However, the bronze plaques on the gate pillars, which recorded the opening of the Gardens in 1927, were saved and are now in North Somerset Museum Service's collections.

Children make a fuss of donkey 'Ginger' on the beach, 24 August 1958. The child riding him is Marilyn Hill. Donkeys have been used on Weston beach for hundreds of years. They were originally used by fishermen to haul their catch up from their boats. As the first visitors arrived in the late eighteenth century, they would hire the donkeys for excursions to nearby villages, and so the concept of donkey rides at the seaside was born.

Holidaymaker writing a postcard home. The corner of Knightstone Causeway and the Promenade, 10 July 1958.

Birnbeck Pier with one of P & A Campbell's steamers at the jetty, 13 August 1953. In the foreground, a workman is up a ladder replacing a light bulb in a street lamp. The lifeboat slipway is Britain's longest at 112.8 metres, to take account of the very high rise and fall of the tide here – the second highest in the world.

An aerial view of Birnbeck Pier with P & A Campbell's paddle steamer *Glen Usk* at the jetty, 14 August 1959. This clearly shows the buildings on the island, including the two pavilions and clock tower. Just to the north of the lifeboat house, is an older lifeboat house, built in 1889. It was replaced with the present building in 1902.

Bathers enjoy the Open Air Pool, August 1954. This concrete diving stage, built in 1937, was one of Weston's most distinctive features until its demolition in 1982. This was due to its becoming unsafe and concerns over the depth of water underneath. At one time it was used for elaborate synchronised diving displays.

The front of the Open Air Pool before the façade was altered to take shop windows, 29 August 1968. In 1983 the pool became the Tropicana, a pleasure beach complex with water slides and splash pools. It is currently closed whilst plans are considered for its future.

One of the pleasure boats comes in to land on Weston Sands, 20 August 1958. These huge wooden landing stages were used up until the 1960s. After that period, boats continued to land and embark at Anchor Head but not on the main beach. The boats used were flatners, a local craft with a flat bottom to enable it to beach without tilting over. They also had a minimal draught and could be sailed in very shallow of water.

Madeira Cove from Glentworth Hall. This view clearly shows the colonnade around Marine Lake. This was so badly damaged in the great storm of 1981 that it had to be demolished. The Model Railway can be seen housed in the Cove Pavilion, once the setting for Pierrot shows. Further along the bay is the Rozel Bandstand.

Marine Lake and Coronation Gardens, August 1954. This is a view of the same area as in the picture above, but viewed from Knightstone. The word Pierrots can be seen on the Cove Pavilion, set amidst shrubs and flowers, presumably planted to commemorate the coronation of Queen Elizabeth II the previous year. The spire of Holy Trinity church marks the centre of the area once known as Cliftonville.

Dredging and levelling the sand and silt in Marine Lake, May 1958. The build-up of silt has been a constant problem here since the causeway was built in 1927. It was constructed to create a bay where 'the tide was always in', and was quite a feat of engineering for its day.

Playing giant draughts at Knightstone, 22 August 1955. In the background is another view of the Rozel Bandstand, with tiers of seating above, rising to Birnbeck Road. This was used for band and organ concerts throughout the summer season. It too was a casualty of the 1981 storm and had to be demolished.

Two boys prepare to launch their craft on the boating pool on the sands, Whit Monday 26 May 1958.

Punch and Judy show on the Beach, 14 August 1952. Punch & Judy shows have long been an essential feature of the seaside. In Weston, the Staddon family were perhaps the most famous operators, but the tradition is continued today with the latest operator being Mr Steve Walker.

Bank Holiday crowds on the sands and promenade, 1971. It is rare to see quite so many people today. Note the man on the promenade in the centre, who has made a sun hat from his newspaper.

THE CHARM AND BEAUTY OF ALL
BRITAIN IN HALF-AN-ACRE OF
DELIGHTFULLY LANDSCAPED ROCK
GARDENS AND INCORPORATING
SOME OF THE FINEST ARCHITECTURAL
MODELS IN THE COUNTRY

Illuminated at Dusk

THE VILLAGE OF COMPTON FIDDLESTIX

'LITTLE BRITAIN'

MODEL VILLAGE

ROYAL PARADE, WESTON-SUPER-MARE
(ADJOINING WINTER GARDENS)

THE MANOR HOUSE

OPEN ALL THE YEAR
Summer 10 a.m. - 10 p.m.
Winter 10 a.m. - Dusk

'LITTLE BRITAIN' will obviously appeal
to party organisers and you are
invited to apply for the generous
party reductions

HOME FARM

Advertisement for Little Britain Model Village. This was built in 1962 on land belonging to the Royal Hotel, just next to Spider Lane. It cost £10,000 to build, and provided entertainment to visitors until 1986, when, after repeated vandalism, it was dismantled and sold. Some of the buildings can still be seen at the Castle Café in Kewstoke.

The foyer of the Royal Hotel, 8 January 1964. This was the first hotel in the town, opening in 1810. It has undergone many alterations and enlargements over the years, with this section of the building dating to the 1840s.

The Royal Hotel and Model Village from the roof of the Winter Gardens. The oldest part of the hotel is the block to the right, with the arched veranda. The curved ballroom and conference room was built in 1961. The 'Royalty Room' as it was called, was opened by beauty queen, Miss Weston-super-Mare, who rode into the room on a Weston donkey.

The Queen's Hotel on the corner of Regent Street and Union Street, 6 November 1960, the building was demolished as part of the town centre developments shortly after this photograph was taken. The site is now occupied by Superdrug. The small box in the middle of the road was for a police officer on point duty, directing traffic.

The Upper Lounge of the Queen's Hotel, 14 May 1960.

The Cambridge Hotel, Beach Road, 2 October 1957. This shows two of Weston's earliest seafront houses, although the right-hand building has undergone substantial alterations over the years. The post on the right once supported cables for the trams that ran along Beach Road.

The dining room of the Welbeck Hotel, corner of Greenfield Place and Knightstone Road, 8 August 1964. This photograph could almost date from the 1930s, so little appears to have been changed since then.

The new Tourist Information Centre on Beach Lawns was opened on 23 October 1973 by Sir Mark Henig, Chairman of the English Tourist Board. He was greeted with a fanfare from trumpeters from RAF Locking, as he arrived in a pony and trap. The building cost £20,000 to construct.

The interior of the new Tourist Information Centre, with its 24ft long split-level counter. In 1974, staff dealt with over 7,000 enquiries, mainly regarding accommodation, but also about places to visit and travel information.

Two

Trade

The shop window of A. & E. Moore's fruit shop, Magdala Buildings, Walliscote Road, pictured on 10 March 1961, appears to be in a time-warp. It could just as easily be 1931. The baskets of fruit are beautifully arranged, backed with alternating red and white grapes hung from the rail.

Betteridge's pram shop in Oxford Street, 11 June 1966. The attractive glass over the main windows has adverts for Silver Cross and Pedigree, two well-known makes of perambulators. On the right is the Oxford Street post office and on the left, Millers' music shop.

The Thrift Shop, Orchard Street, 3 April 1972. Discount and charity shops are so common nowadays, that it is hard to believe they were once a novelty.

The new shop front for Good Cheer Cellars, at 333 Locking Road, on 6 July 1961.

Cabinet Handicraft Supplies, Orchard Place, 31 October 1962. Amongst the goods on display in this window is Liden whitewood furniture. Before the days of MDF and melamine, whitewood furniture was a cheap and practical alternative. Since it was unfinished you could decorate it in your taste with paint or varnish.

Steed Colour TV Centre, Waterloo Street, 29 May 1973. Colour televisions were still very much a novelty at this time, not to mention expensive.

The interior of Steed Colour TV Centre in Waterloo Street. As you can see, as well as televisions, the shop also sold radiograms, a mains-powered combined radio and record player – a far cry from the micro and mini-systems popular today.

Painting the unique decorative lead façade of W.H. Smith & Son, High Street, early 1960s. The wording at the top reads 'Come and take choice of all my library and so beguile thy sorrow'. After some years of neglect, this façade and the attractive wooden bay windows were restored in 1999.

The window display at Phillput's Ltd, The Boulevard, 5 October 1963 celebrates sixty-five years of Parker Pens. Phillput's was a well-known stationers, supplying many businesses until its closure in the 1980s.

Husbands' camera shop, High Street South, 16 February 1961. An array of darkroom equipment is displayed in the lower half of the window with a wide range of cameras above. Next door, Radio Rentals are offering one month's rental free on their television sets.

Salisbury's handbag and luggage shop, High Street, 9 March 1961. On the right of Salisbury's is Marks & Spencer, whilst on the left is Hosken & Co, wholesale and retail tobacconists.

Drivers toy shop, Waterloo Street, 8 March 1966. Drivers began in 1903 when Mr Walter Driver and Mr S. Feaver came to Weston from Birmingham. Their first shop was opposite the Playhouse and sold prams, toys, bicycles, motorcycles and also had an agency for the Model T Ford. The business moved to this shop in 1906 and traded here until the building was damaged by bombs in 1941. They moved back into this shop in 1948, moving again into one of the new shops built in Waterloo Street on the site of Lance & Lance. Here they continued trading until 1971, when the business was sold. Today this building is Papa's Fish and Chip shop.

Mr E.W. Denner's antique shop, Orchard Street, 2 August 1956. The shop on the left, John Kemp, Groceries and Provisions, looks as if it belongs in the Victorian era. What a wonderful window display of tins, packets and boxes of biscuits.

Stokes Motors, Orchard Street pictured here on 11 July 1972, were 'Dealers in Quality Cars and Vans', according to the description in the Kelly's Directory. The showroom was built in what once were gardens backing the properties in the Boulevard.

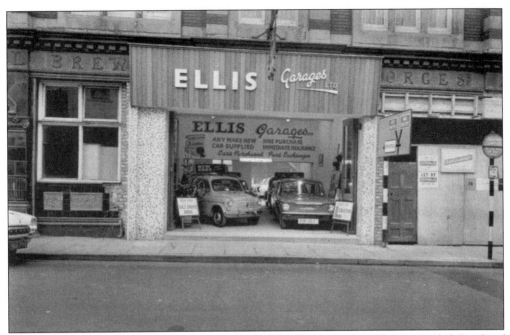

Ellis Garages Ltd, Regent Street, 16 December 1963. Here, the fine Victorian tiled façade of the Plough Hotelhas been broken up and this car showroom built in the resulting space. The whole site is now occupied by Marks & Spencer's Regent Street extension.

Another view of Ellis Garages Ltd, 5 August 1963. This view shows the Plough Hotel Yard area. The whole of the Plough Hotel, including this part, was demolished when the extension to Marks & Spencer's was built in the 1980s.

The sign on the wall of the butcher's shop in Dolphin Square market on 2 March 1969 reads, 'Farm Bred Rabbits', not a common sight today. Other stalls here are selling fruit, vegetables and cream cakes. Today the market sells mainly cheap clothing and household goods.

Atkinson's Electrical shop, Dolphin Square, 1 March 1973. The poster on the right-hand window reads 'Beat the Gas Strike – keep warm with an electric heater, £3.75'. On the left the hairdresser's is offering Green Shield Stamps and on the right is Curry & Paxton's opticians.

The furniture department of Cashman's DIY store, 30 August 1973. Cashman's was in the old tram shed in Locking Road behind what is now the RSPCA office. They sold a wide variety of goods, from garden equipment and carpets to kitchens and bathrooms.

The showroom at Payne & Holder, Whitecross Road, 4 November 1959. As well as furniture, such as the pouffes, chairs and wardrobes, Payne & Holder also sold electrical goods such as radios and televisions.

The Calor Gas showroom, Rector's Way, 26 August 1975. In October 2000, planning permission was sought to build homes on this site.

The walkway between Boots' and Colmer's shops, High Street, 14 November 1967. This was a very useful shortcut between the shops, especially if it was raining. In addition you could leave Colmer's through a door into Cambridge Place and nip into Woolworth's through a door opposite, barely getting wet at all.

Colmer's Christmas Grotto, 18 November 1965. This shop was originally B.T. Butter's, one of Weston's oldest shops, opening in the High Street in 1847. In 1911 they acquired the properties next door as far as Cambridge Place and expanded accordingly. It was taken over by Colmer's in 1946.

An autumn display of Berketex clothing in Colmer's window, High Street, 21 October 1961. In 1973 Colmer's became part of the Owen Owen Group and traded as such until they closed in 1993. This shop was demolished and Abbey National and Etam now occupy the new building.

The Pittard's glove display in Colmer's, High Street, 12 May 1965. One has to wonder how they got away with the uncovered fuse box on the right, with the hand-written sign 'Danger 260 Volts'!

A display of Van-Dal Norfolk Broads shoes in Scudamore's Shoe Shop, Waterloo Street, 28 April 1961.

The interior of Trend, West Street pictured on 25 October 1974, is packed full of those 1970s essentials – ropes of beads, dyed ostrich feathers and Pre-Raphaelite prints.

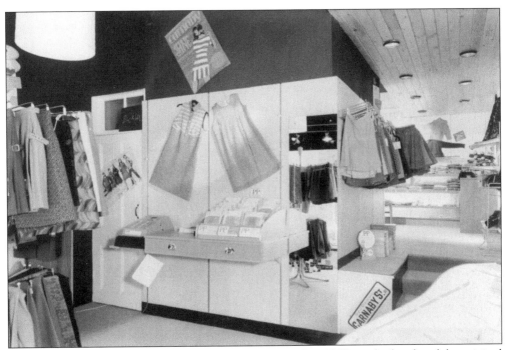

The interior of Carnaby Jane, St James Street, 5 December 1967, at the height of the original miniskirt era!

Mr Weeks, weighing out coffee in Carwardine's High Street shop, 16 May 1966. The most wonderful aromas of roasting coffee used to float down the High Street from Carwardine's tempting you into their small café at the back of the shop.

Sale time at Marks & Spencer, 31 July 1958. These dresses are on sale for 40s.

The interior of the café at Astill & Son's bakery, West Street, 18 May 1972, which was in an upstairs room and closed around 1985.

The Monte Carlo Restaurant, St James Street, 17 April 1963.

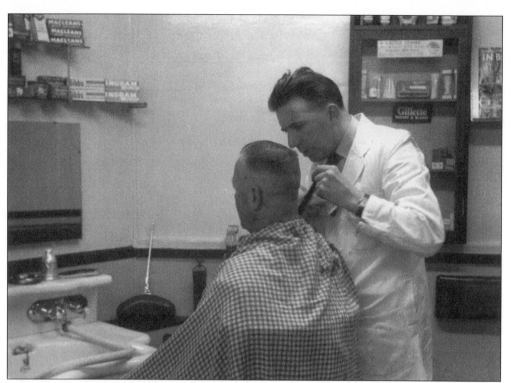

W.J. Amesbury cutting Bill Shenton's hair in Amesbury's Hairdressing Salon, April 1958. This salon was at 10 Meadow Street.

The interior of the new salon of Bernard of Mayfair, Waterloo Street, 17 June 1959. Mr Bernard is standing to the right. The décor evokes the period wonderfully, with the padded and quilted vinyl, chandeliers and white wrought iron.

Three
Industry

Mr J. Smout making Procea bread at Perrett's Bakery, 61 High Street, 22 June 1958. Procea was a low calorie type of bread.

H.E. Bryant's ironmongers, Oxford Street, 17 August 1958. Bill Shenton is seen working on a wrought iron glass door grill in the blacksmith's shop at the rear of the premises.

Antar tank carriers being overhauled at Henlys Ltd, Oldmixon, July 1958. Henlys Ltd were the contractors to the Ministry of Supply from 1948 until 1965. They repaired, reconditioned and overhauled a wide range of military vehicles for all three services.

Mr L. Reasons of the Bristol Aeroplane Company, Oldmixon, at work in the cockpit of a helicopter, 1958. At this time, the company was the largest single employer in the whole of the West Country, and one of the world's largest aviation firms. At this site, in addition to helicopters, the firm also made prefabricated aluminium buildings and components for the Bristol Britannia airliner.

A Bristol Helicopter, type 173, at the Bristol Aeroplane Company factory at Oldmixon, 29 May 1958. This aircraft was the world's first twin-engined helicopter to offer safe flight on only one engine. As a result, there were large Government orders which required an extension of the factory assembly lines, creating many more jobs.

Compositor, Jack Dando making up a page for the *Weston Mercury & Somerset Herald* newspaper, 26 April 1958. Jack was in charge of the composing room at the Mercury until his retirement in 1984. He is the father of TV presenter, Jill Dando who was tragically murdered in 1999.

At Lawrence Brothers, printers on North Street, 5 May 1958 Miss A. Merryweather is seen setting up one of the machines. Lawrence Brothers started up in Weston in the nineteenth century as stationers, bookbinders and printers.

The line of printing machines at Lawrence Allen Ltd, Gloucester Street, 29 June 1972. This firm started as Lawrence Brothers (see above photograph) in the late nineteenth century and is still operating, but is now based in Bristol.

W. Neame examining a pocket watch in the workshop of Leonard Couch, jewellers, St James Street, 5 February 1957. This photograph by C.A. Pople was awarded first prize in the Advanced Section of the monthly competition for Weston Camera Club in 1957.

Testing men's shoes at the Whitecross Road shoe factory of C. & J. Clark Ltd, 10 July 1958. When Clarks moved to a new factory in Locking Road, this site was taken over by Peggy Nisbet Ltd, makers of costume and historical dolls. It is now a dance studio.

Shoemaker Mr H. Baker, one of Weston's old master craftsmen, at work at Messrs T.H. Jeffries, Orchard Street, 1958. He is seen stitching the sole on a man's shoe.

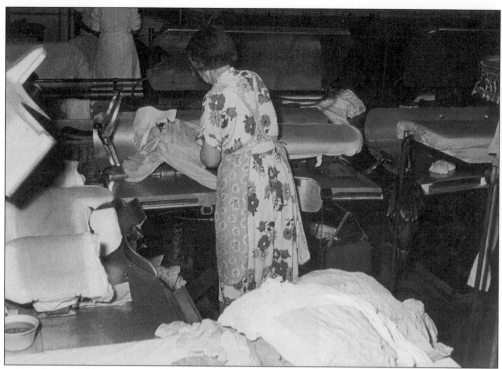

The pressing machine at Moorland Laundry, Moorland Road, August 1958. There was always a lot of work for laundries in a holiday resort, catering for all the hotels and guest houses.

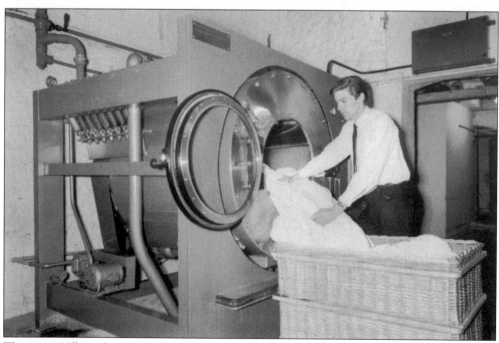

The new 100lb washer extractor at the Imperial Laundry, Worle, 1 February 1969.

The exterior of Ansal Mosaics Ltd, Winterstoke Road, 7 March 1964. As can be seen by the lettering on the building, this was originally the Royal Pottery. Founded in the 1830s in Locking Road, the Pottery moved to this site in the 1890s, as land for clay digging at the old site ran out. They specialised in clay garden wares, but also made bricks and roof tiles. The firm closed in 1961. This building can still be seen today with its faded lettering.

Removing molten glass from the furnace at Ansal Mosaics, Winterstoke Road, 9 March 1964.

The motor room at Black Rock pumping station, Windwhistle Road, 27 September 1962, just before it was officially opened. It was designed to prevent a recurrence of the serious flooding that inundated the centre of the town in 1949. All the machinery was below ground level, with just the transformer station and crane system above ground.

The motor floor with mural, Black Rock pumping station, Windwhistle Road, 27 September 1962. This room contained three 58hp constant-speed electric motors, driving pumps capable of discharging 4,000 gallons per minute against the maximum spring tide. Additional motors could be brought on line to deal with storm flow. The striking modern mural was designed and executed by the Borough Engineer's painting and decorating staff.

Four
Our Changing Town

Men painting white lines by hand in the High Street, 1958. Opposite is the window of Colmer's, whilst to the left of Cambridge Place, Woolworth's is advertising Easter Cards.

The High Street North, early 1960s. This block of buildings is called Somerset House, and was designed by local architect, Hans Price in 1897. Mr Gibson's shop was amalgamated into the frontage of the Playhouse Theatre shortly after this picture was taken (see top photograph on p59). Originally it was Fox's Japanese Bazaar and sported a larger-than-life Japanese figure of a woman over the window.

The High Street from Regent Street, 30 May 1973. The few shoppers out on this wet day are huddled under the shop blinds. At this time, the High Street was still open to motor traffic, albeit one way.

The High Street, 1973. This shows a busy day, later in the year than the previous picture, when work had started to make the High Street into a pedestrian precinct. In November that year, all vehicles were banned completely. A wide variety of architectural styles is shown on these mostly Victorian buildings.

The Royal Chambers, on the corner of West Street and High Street North, 17 February 1962. This site originally held Weston's Assembly Rooms. Built in 1859, the style was described as Venetian Italian. There were seven shops on the ground floor with a large assembly room on the first floor. The room was used for concerts, dances and public meetings. Unfortunately it suffered a direct hit during the Second World War.

Dolphin Square shopping precinct, 1973. This was built as part of a much larger plan to relocate the main shopping area. Since the funding fell through, the rest of the scheme was never built. Many improvements were made to the Square in 1999, including a new entrance and children's play area.

The Playhouse, High Street North, *c.* 1963. This building was originally the Market Hall. In 1946 it was converted into a 500-seat theatre, to provide an additional venue to the theatre at Knightstone. It underwent several improvements over the years until it burnt down in 1964.

On the night of 21 August 1964 the Playhouse suffered a devastating fire. These are the ruins the following day. They reveal the shell of the original market hall, built in 1869 and incorporated into the block of new shops built in the 1890s (see top photograph p56). A new theatre was built and opened in 1969 and is still in use today (see bottom photograph p110).

The High Street South, February 1964. This road was originally Gas Street, as the town's first gasworks were here in the 1840s. Later it became Union Street, before being totally demolished in the late 1950s, widened, and these building erected. In the centre here is the Central Cinema in Oxford Street just before it too was demolished for the Dolphin Square development.

New shops in High Street South, c. 1964. In the distance is the Midland bank, now the HSBC Bank on the corner of High Street and Regent Street.

Advertising hoardings mask one of the demolition sites in Oxford Street, 20 September 1958. This is prior to the redevelopment of the area with Dolphin Square.

Shops in Magdala Buildings, Walliscote Road, c. 1960.

Regent Street at the junction with Meadow Street, May 1952. The policewoman is on point duty, directing the traffic. The whole block of buildings behind her, with the exception of the Railway Hotel on the right seen advertising Georges' Beers, was demolished in a new road traffic scheme in 1966.

The Victoria Hotel, Regent Street, 19 December 1969. This was one of Weston's older inns, built about 1850. It was demolished in 1981 when an extension to the Tesco supermarket was planned. A few years later, Tesco built their present store and the extension was never built. The new General Post Office and Cancer Research Charity shop occupy the site today.

Regent Street looking west towards the Grand Pier, 14 October 1959. On the immediate left is the Gaumont Cinema, one of Weston's then 3 cinemas together with the Odeon and Central. Of these only the Odeon remains.

Regent Street, late 1950s. The Cavendish Hotel, on the left, is now Ebenezer Riley's Front Room, a rather bizarrely-named pub. Bernies Café is advertising Kunzle Cakes. These were made at Clevedon, at the Hales factory.

Regent Street looking east, 19 December 1969. The building on the left was the Railway Hotel, currently Jack Stamps Beer House. None of the buildings in the main part of the picture survive today, the site being occupied by In Shops, B-Wise, the General Post Office and Cancer Research Charity Shop.

Regent Street from the High Street, 30 May 1973. The block in the previous photograph has been demolished and the new building is seen under construction, with the new multi-storey car park just beyond it.

St James Street, late 1950s. This is one of Weston's oldest streets, built in the 1840s and 1850s. Couch's were the stockists of all the local school uniforms and had two shops in this street, one for menswear, and one for ladies and children's wear, separated by the Globe Hotel.

St James Street, c. 1958. Coffin & Sons and Farrs are the two oldest fish and chip shops in Weston, both being established here in the late nineteenth century. The 1866 Directory shows just how much variety of trade there was in this street at one time, listing a dairyman, beer retailer, greengrocer, chemist, butcher, dressmaker, stationer, silk and crepe dyer, watchmaker, dealer in shells, fly proprietor and boot and shoemaker.

The Floral Clock and Regent Street from the roof of the Odeon Cinema, 1 July 1951. This shows the layout before the new road traffic scheme; which meant the demolition of the public toilets just behind the Floral Clock, together with the terrace of three shops just to the right of the Anchor Inn.

Meadow Street, early 1960s. All the buildings on the right side of the road were demolished in 1966 for a new road scheme and one-way system. The Bristol & West Bank occupies part of the site today.

Meadow Street, 1966. The block of shops at the High Street end of Regent Street and Meadow Street has just been demolished as part of the new road scheme, exposing these properties on the north side of Meadow Street.

The back of Regent Street properties after the demolition of Union Street for road-widening and new development. In the distance is the High Street with what is now the HSBC Bank on the corner. The lane on the right was part of Wilcox Place; a court of workshops and cottages which were also demolished at this time.

Moving a piano from the upstairs of 19 Meadow Street, with the mobile crane parked in North Street, 27 March 1958. At this date television was still a novelty and people could often be seen standing in front of this window watching the TV sets.

North Street, looking north towards Palmer Row, 1974. All the buildings on the right hand side of the road went when the road was widened in the late 1970s. The pedestrianization of the High Street meant that North Street became the main delivery access for the shops on the eastern side of the High Street.

Union Street after demolition, with the rear of properties in St James Street. The building on the extreme left was the Three Queens Pub, now called the Pig and Truffles.

Man with a budgerigar near Rector's Way off Drove Road, 1 May 1958. Members of Weston-super-Mare Cage Bird Society held annual shows at the town hall, so could this be where this man is going?

Reeves Cottages, c. 1957. These were up a narrow lane off Carlton Street on the south side and were part of the area cleared in the late 1950s to make way for the planned new development which included a new tower-block hotel, library, shops and flats. As funding fell through, only the Dolphin Square section was built. Carlton Street Car Park now occupies this site.

Carlton Street looking west, c. 1957. The right-hand side of the road is now the rear of the Dolphin Square Market, whilst a car park occupies the left-hand side.

Little Carlton Street looking south. At the end of the road, Carlton Street crosses at right angles, with the small passage beyond leading to Sidmouth Cottages. The sign warns motorists that Walliscote Infant School is just round the corner on the left. Some of these properties are already boarded up and empty prior to demolition.

Carlton Street, looking east along the northern side, with Walliscote Infant School at the end of the road. These elegant seaside villas were built in the mid-nineteenth century.

Demolition of St Heliers, the property on the corner of Carlton Street and Beach Road, *c.* 1960. In the background on the right is the bus station. This was demolished in January 1988 after deregulation of bus services. There has not yet been a replacement.

New Street, looking south to Carlton Street, *c.* 1957. The Prince of Wales pub can just be glimpsed at the end of the road. The lane on the right leads to New Street South. Residents from this area were re-housed in two new blocks of flats built in Milton Road opposite Manor Road, on the site of the Weston, Clevedon & Portishead Light Railway coalyard.

Vegetable gardens of Meadow Villas, 2 March 1961. Across the gardens is Burlington Street with the Gaslight Company Stores, built in 1912. This was converted into a new home for the Museum when Local Government reorganization split the library and museum services in 1974.

Palmer Street from the top of the *Weston Mercury* building, *c.* 1975. This clearly shows the tightly packed terraces of houses built in the 1860s. You can also just see three or four workshops, built in the gardens of some of the houses. These were used for a variety of trades and were reached by arched alleyways running between some of the houses.

The backs of properties in Palmer Row, photographed from the top of the *Weston Mercury* building, *c.* 1975.

Palmer Row, 1975. This old stable, belonging to the White Hart Inn opposite, was used for many years by local fishermen to sell their catch. You could call here and buy a pound or two of freshly caught sprats or dabs, up until the late 1980s.

Orchard Street, 11 June 1972. This mid-Victorian building is on the Southwest corner of Burlington Street. It was used here as an antiquarian bookshop, but has since been altered and is now Pet and Pond Supplies.

This small cottage at 22 Orchard Street, has an original mid-Victorian shop front. Since this photograph was taken on 9 May 1979, the building has been incorporated into the Working Men's club on the left.

Alfred Street, looking north towards the Boulevard, 1975. The wooden sign on the property in the centre is for H.J. Norton & Sons, Monumental Masons.

Nos 21 and 22 Beach Road were the home of the Somerset County Council fire brigade for a few years. Their original station was in Oxford Street but that building had to be vacated when the street was marked for redevelopment. The brigade moved from this site to their present fire station at the end of Milton Avenue when it was opened in 1960.

These old cottages in Gloucester Street, seen here in 1976, have to be some of Weston's oldest cottages, probably dating from the 1840s.

South Parade, photographed from the Winter Gardens putting green, 5 October 1974. The Imperial Hotel was originally the Bath Hotel, built in 1819. This was Weston's second hotel, built nine years after the Royal Hotel opened.

A view of the Grosvenor Hotel and Royal Terrace, 19 May 1967, from the site of St John's School. The school had been demolished the previous year to make way for the new Technical College now Weston College. In addition to the school, a terrace of seven houses was also cleared to make way for the eight-storey college.

St John's School in Lower Church Road, shown on the left here, was built in 1845 as the National School. This Church of England school charged pupils 2d per week, or 1d if more than one child from a family attended. The school later became St John's School, finally closing in 1964. The site is now occupied by Weston College.

Weston Grammar School, c. 1963. This school opened in 1936 and was effectively two schools, the Grammar School for Girls on the left, and the Grammar School for Boys on the right, the children being taught in single-sex classes. It later became Broadoak School, and was demolished in October 1999 when a new building opened on what were formerly the playing fields.

The School of Science and Art, Lower Church Road, c. 1975. This was built in 1897 and was designed by local architect, Hans Price. In 1975 it was used as the Art Department of Weston Technical College, situated behind it. The Technical College opened in 1970 and was built entirely of concrete. It cost £1million and catered for 1,400 full-time students. Over recent years it has been extended and has undergone a complete facelift.

Weston Decorators Supply Ltd Boulevard, 27 August 1971. This building was on the corner of Orchard Street and is now a café and bistro. In this picture the building is for sale prior to the firm's move, further up the road, to its current premises.

A wet day in the Boulevard, 6 February 1968. This end of the street is now mostly occupied by hairdressers and beauty salons. At the time of the photograph there was a greengrocer, baker's and sweet shop, as well as the Gas Board Showroom.

Waterloo Street from an upper window of Norman, Wright & Co.'s offices, 1 November 1958. The open site was created when Lance & Lance was hit by incendiary bombs in 1942, and is being used as a car park.

By the 1 July 1960 a new block of shops on Waterloo Street, built on the car park site in the above photograph, had been partially completed. Only the corner building, now Argos, had yet to be built.

This elegant Edwardian house on Clarence Road North, was demolished in the 1970s and redeveloped as a block of flats. Chandos Court now occupies the site.

'The Turret' on Grove Park Road is still standing today, but at some date between 24 July 1962 and 1980 the rather attractive turret was removed and a flat roof created on the corner bay windows.

Upper Church Road looking west, 25 June 1976. The terrace on the right was built in the 1850s, and the remainder of the road built in the 1880s. The whole road was residential until the late 1880s, when the ground floors began to be converted into shops. Just over the roofline are Villa Rosa flats, built in 1972.

Shrubbery Garage, Upper Church Road, was originally built as a mews for the livery of horses and carriages. In 1986 it was demolished and a row of town houses built.

The ruins of the Boulevard Congregational church, 14 May 1957 show the state of the church after it received a direct hit during the Second World War. A new church, built on the original foundations, was opened in 1959.

St Paul's church in Walliscote Road was another Weston church destroyed by enemy action in January 1941. This photograph shows rebuilding in progress during 1956. Services continued to be held in the south aisle, until the church's re-consecration in 1957.

Building St Peter's Church, Milton, 12 December 1964 on the corner of Baytree Road and Locking Road. The church was designed in the Scandinavian Gothic style, and is the only church in the area that breaks with Christian tradition and is aligned north-south, rather than east-west. The tower was removed in 1991 when it became unsafe.

St Andrews church, Bournville was opened in 1957 in order to replace a small wooden chapel on the same site. In June 2000, it was announced that the church would be demolished to make way for a new community complex housing a doctor's surgery, hall, day centre, café and church.

Glentworth Court flats, pictured on 15 March 1978, replaced Glentworth Hall, a large mansion built in the 1840s. In the background on the left is Raglan Terrace in Upper Church Road. This terrace was being built during the Crimean War when news arrived that the Allied Commander, Lord Raglan's body was to be brought up the Bristol Channel by boat that day in 1855. It was because of that event that the name Raglan Terrace was chosen.

St Andrew's Parade in Lonsdale Avenue, Bournville pictured on 17 October 1975 replaced the temporary shops set up in Nissen huts after the Second World War.

The kitchen of a show bungalow on the County Estate, Ewart Road, 8 November 1957. Some of the ideas in this kitchen seem quite modern, with the eye-level built-in refrigerator. The kitchen had blue tiles, a red centre panel in the floor and grey doors.

New detached houses on the Corondale Estate, 23 August 1965. The right-hand house has a new price of £3,500 in the upper window.

Ashcombe Park Putting Course, 15 June 1953. This park was formally opened in 1902 and, at thirty-six acres, is the largest in Weston. When the land was acquired in the 1880s, there were few trees. The planting was planned to accentuate the hillside with its dramatic views and includes a Lime Walk winding up the shallow combe and a row of sycamores.

Clarence Park tea room, 10 July 1962. This appears to have been a popular meeting place for young mothers. The land for Clarence Park was donated in 1882 by Rebecca Davies, widow of William Davies, a local property speculator of the mid-nineteenth century.

The South Gallery at the Museum, Boulevard, 1954. These two ladies are looking at a display of finds from Worlebury Iron Age Hillfort. In the background is the fossilised skeleton of an ichthyosaur, still on display today in the museum in Burlington Street.

Weston Library, Boulevard, c. 1957. In 2000 this building celebrated its centenary.

Oxford Street from the Centre Café, 20 July 1958. The Town Hall is on the left. The interesting-looking shop on the right is Northy-Baker & Co. Ltd, herbalists, tobacconists, fancy goods and photographic dealers.

Station Road, 23 August 1968. Lalonde's furniture depository and auction rooms, with the tower of the Victoria Methodist church to the right. The business of auctioneers and estate agents, Norton, Son & Lalonde, was established in 1848, the first of its kind in Weston. The building is used by Nightingale's Removals today.

A northbound passenger train leaves Weston Station in the 1960s. Weston Signal Box can be seen on the left. The tracks to the right lead to the excursion platforms, whilst those in the centre lead to the goods yard. The majority of this area is now occupied by Locking Road car park.

Weston Goods Yard, c.1958. A 61XX class 2-6-2 T Great Western Railway locomotive is being cleaned. These engines were designed by C.B. Collett and were introduced in 1931. They were mainly used for suburban passenger trains.

Locking Road looking west, 4 October 1966. The building on the left was Weston's first excursion station built in 1854. All the buildings in the picture were demolished shortly after this picture was taken.

Weston Goods Station, 1982. This station was built in 1862, to cater for the ever-increasing amounts of freight sent to and from Weston. When the new through station was built in 1883, the old passenger station became the Goods Station and this building was used for other purposes. It was demolished in 1984 and the site is now occupied by Hildesheim Court and Tesco's supermarket.

Weston Goods Yard from the Odeon Cinema, 1970s. This is a good overview of the yard after the decline in freight traffic. The building in the foreground is the Excursion Station and platforms, built in 1914. Centre right is part of the old 1866 passenger station, used for goods since 1883 and bombed during the Second World War. Behind that is the back of the 1862 Goods Station, (see bottom photograph p94).

Entrance to the Goods Yard, 1976. This was once the Excursion Station, but with the decline of excursion trains due to the rise in car ownership and coaches, it was used for a time as the Goods Yard Office before its demolition in 1984 to make way for the new Tesco supermarket.

Control Tower, Weston Airport, 14 September 1959. The building in the distance, to the left, was the passenger terminal, opened in June 1936 when air travel was very much a novelty. The following year, at Whitsun, over 2,555 passengers travelled from Weston Airport – a world record at that time.

An Auster aircraft with pilot Peter Lucas, at Weston Airport, 21 June 1961.

Five

People in Uniform

An exercise at the fire station in Beach Road (see top photograph p78), 25 June 1957. From left to right are firemen E. Hibbert, W. Doades, S. Venn.

The Citizens Advice Bureau in the High Street, February 1961. On the right is the National Westminster Bank, whilst on the left is Pages, a shop specialising in handbags, luggage and leather goods.

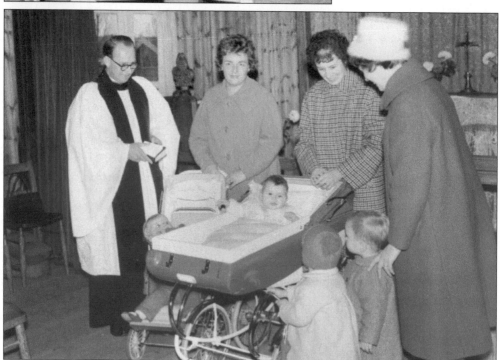

The Revd Costello at a pram service at St Peter's church, Baytree Road, 2 November 1962. A small wooden mission hut was used at this date, but as soon as sufficient funds were raised, the present church was built and opened in 1965 (see top photograph p87).

Council refuse collectors in St James Street, 15 April 1958. From left to right: W. Davis, J. Keirle, S. Reid, B. Adams.

Council employees removing the tarmac from the High Street, prior to resurfacing, in 1958. They have exposed the old wood blocks that once paved many of the main streets. These blocks are still *in situ* but the only place you can see such a surface today is in the courtyard of the Museum in Burlington Street, where they were laid in the 1860s when the building was a mews.

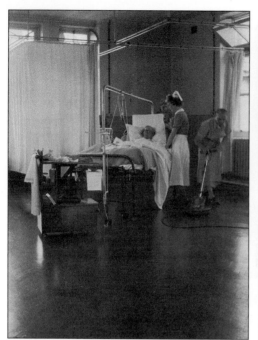
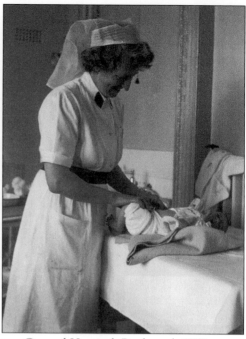

Left: Cleaning the Jackson-Barstow ward at Weston General Hospital, Boulevard, 1958.
Right: Sister Bidmead, changing a baby at Ashcombe House Maternity Hospital, 1958. Built in the 1850s for the Capell family, this building was used as a Red Cross Hospital during the First World War. It then became a Maternity Hospital until the present unit opened in 1986.

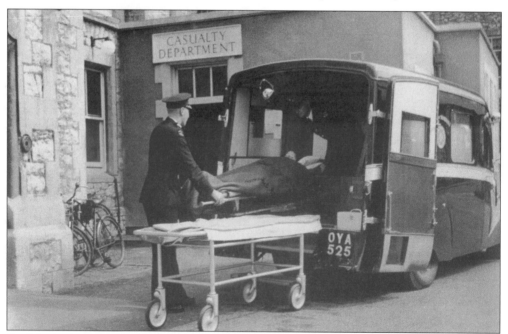

St John's Ambulancemen delivering a patient to Weston General Hospital Casualty Department, Alfred Street, 1958. Left is Brian Parfitt and right is Dennis Cotgrove. After the new General Hospital opened in 1986, these buildings were converted for residential use.

Six

Entertainment

The Vernon Adcock Show at the Rozel Bandstand, 20 June 1965. Vernon Adcock was born in Birmingham and worked with the Birmingham Symphony Orchestra. He also worked on BBC Radio with his own orchestra in 1945 before coming to Weston. He then embarked on a thirty-year career here, playing both at the Winter Gardens and the Rozel Bandstand until his retirement in 1986.

Billy Smart's Circus arriving in Locking Road, June 1956. The circus set up in Locking with a 6,000-seater big top from 19 June 1956 for one week. As well as these 'Dancing Elephants', there were over 200 animals, including lions, polar bears and camels. They also advertised a special Western Spectacle with Cowboys and Indians. Today there are no circuses in Britain featuring wild animals in this way.

The Summer Carnival, June 1958. This was the first carnival to be held for twenty years. The procession was followed by an ox-roast on Beach Lawns with a Carnival Dance at the Winter Gardens that evening when the prizes were presented.

The local detachment of the Territorial Army in the Marine Lake on Saturday 17 May 1958, at the end of the Wessex Royal Engineer's (TA) inter-squadron contests. It was won by the 205th Field Squadron (Weston).

The Soap Box Derby, Weston sea front, 8 September 1956. These go-carts were built by local scouts and raced annually for many years.

Weston Chrysanthemum Show at the Winter Gardens, 4 November 1952. Sheeting has been put down to protect the wooden dance floor. The magnificent display at the top of the steps was put on by the Council's Parks Department. Chrysanthemum shows have been held in Weston since 1882, and are still going strong today.

Ballroom dancing display at the Winter Gardens, televised for the BBC's *Come Dancing* programme, 13 August 1954.

Pupils at the Mavdor School of Dancing, September 1958. From left to right: Katrina Abbott, Jennifer Hillier, Angela Stocker, Jean Causier, Angela Mackenzie, Miss Mavis James (teacher).

Jiving to Modern Jazz at Club 13, RAF Association Club, Grove Road, 24 July 1958.

Group at Ashcombe Bowling Club, Ashcombe Park, 4 June 1960.

Ladies bowling at Ashcombe Bowling Club, 15 June 1953. The Victorian pavilion was once one of the seafront shelters on Weston Promenade.

Water Polo match between Weston A team and Cheltenham A team at Knightstone Baths, 29 July 1957. Left to right: L.A.S. Reed (Weston), -?- (Cheltenham), Buster Hillman (Weston), -?- (Cheltenham).

Bristol Aeroplane Company's Second XI play Banwell at the Baytree Road Recreation Ground, 27 September 1958.

The Odeon Cinema, 2 March 1957. The film showing is *Love me Tender* starring Elvis Presley. This cinema was built in 1935, the last of Weston's three cinemas to be constructed. On the extreme left is a brick building, once the stables for the Great Western Railway, who operated horse-drawn delivery carts for many years.

Roy Pearce practising at the magnificent Compton Organ in the Odeon Cinema, 1 July 1951. This organ has been restored recently and there are frequent recitals today.

The Advance Booking Office at the Gaumont Cinema, Regent Street, 19 July 1960. The Gaumont Cinema, then called the Regent, opened in 1913 when it had its own orchestra to accompany silent films. In 1954 it was renamed the Gaumont and was closed as a cinema in 1973 when it became a Bingo Hall. It was demolished in the 1980s.

The new Sweet Kiosk at the Odeon Cinema, 7 May 1956. On the right you can just see the original mirrored panelling installed in most Odeon Cinemas to make the foyer look larger and more impressive.

Mr Harman, manager of the Gaumont Cinema rides a bicycle between the rows of seats at the cinema, 1 April 1960. He was demonstrating the increased legroom created by re-arranging the seating. These alterations allowed 3ft spaces between rows, although 140 seats were lost in the process. Other improvements at this time included an additional men's toilet and redecoration.

The foyer at the new Playhouse, 17 June 1969. This theatre was built to replace the original one which burnt down in 1964 (see both photographs p59). It is still in use today and has recently undergone refurbishment to make it accessible for the disabled.

Bandleader, Trevor Brookes with his orchestra outside the Winter Gardens, 31 July 1954. The event was a fund-raiser for the St John Ambulance Brigade.

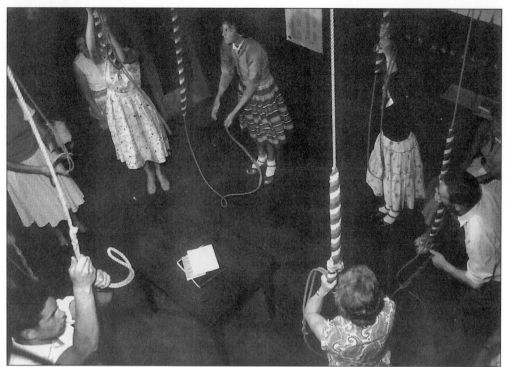

Young members of the Parish church bell-ringers, August 1958. For a time in the 1970s, a tape recording replaced the sounds of real bells at St John's church, but the bell ringers are back today.

A darts game in progress at the Weston British Legion Club, Orchard Street, c. 1958. From left to right: Mr Baker, R. Hancock, Stan Maynard (Alley Attendant), -?-, C. Ashman, -?-, -?-, Tom Pemlott, Mrs Gerry.

Seven
Special Events

Cake made by Perrett's Bakery for the 21st Anniversary of the granting of the Borough Charter to Weston-super-Mare, 20 September 1958. A week of celebrations climaxed in a day of events attended by Lord Alexander, the wartime First Lord of the Admiralty who was born in George Street, Weston. This cake, donated by Perretts, was given to Weston Hospital by the Mayor and Mayoress.

Players from Charlton Athletic Football Club in the foyer of the Odeon Cinema, 8 January 1960. The children are all members of the Odeon's Boys and Girls Club, and had gathered to wish the team good luck for the FA Cup.

Weston actor, Tony Britten opening the Hospital Gardens Fete, 25 July 1959. The event was held on the tennis courts in the centre of the hospital grounds. All the £237 proceeds went to the Hospital League of Friends who used it to create a special relatives room at the hospital.

Mrs Dorothy Bingham-Hall of Glebe House, Weston, with a Nigerian student at the Mayor's Luncheon, 22 May 1958. This event followed the mayor-making ceremony and was held in the town hall.

A car after an unfortunate collision with the frontage of Saturley Garner's window, the Boulevard, 1 December 1963. The Building's previous use as a church can be seen from the glimpse of an arched window over the fascia board. The Boulevard Methodist church was built in 1875 and remained in use until 1959 when it was converted for commercial use.

The mayor, Cllr Holcombe and mayoress, Miss Ruth Holcombe, land in a locally-made helicopter on Beach Lawns for the opening of the Battle of Britain Exhibition, 10 September, 1956. The Bristol Sycamore craft was piloted by J. Williamson.

The Weston-super-Mare branch of the British Legion march up Station Road at the Battle of Britain Parade, 1958. In the background is the old railway engine shed.

HRH Princess Margaret outside Weston Grammar School, 23 May 1953. From left to right: Alderman Mrs M. Miller-Barstow (mayoress), Princess Margaret, Alderman D. Miller-Barstow (mayor), R.G. Lickfold (town clerk), Iris Peake (lady in waiting), Lord Hylton (Lord Lieutenant of Somerset).

Princess Margaret's car passing the Odeon Cinema during her visit to Weston, 23 May 1953. Arriving by aeroplane at Weston Airport, she spent the day visiting a variety of youth organizations, including the cadets at RAF Locking and Weston Grammar School, where she 'was confronted by more children than I have ever seen before'.

The Floral Clock, Alexandra Parade, 1953. The flowers for this design were planted to commemorate the Coronation of Queen Elizabeth II. The clock was first installed in 1935 but did not have a cuckoo until 1951.

A Street Party in Farm Road, 17 June 1977. This was the 25th Jubilee year of the Queen's accession to the throne and celebrations such as this were held all over the country.

The finalists of the Miss TWW (Television Wales & West) beauty competition, 30 August 1963.The event was held in the Winter Gardens pavilion. Beauty pageants were very popular at this time, whether regional ones such as this one, nation-wide ones such as Miss England or world-wide ones like Miss World.

Entrants in the Modern Venus beauty competition at the Open Air Pool, Thursday 24 July 1958. On the right is Mr H. White, deputy superintendent of the pool.

Deck chairs and stage set out for the Marilyn Monroe look-a-like contest, Weston beach, 2 September 1957. This event was organized by the *Sunday Pictorial* newspaper.

The Odeon Cinema, 23 December 1958. The mayor, Cllr L. Holtby is pictured with Mr Bigwood, manager of the cinema, looking at the gifts collected for underprivileged children and old age pensioners.

Mr L. Harman, manager of the Gaumont Cinema, putting gifts on the Christmas tree at St Margaret's Home for children, 23 December 1958.

Eight

Outer Weston

The Castle post office, Worlebury Hill Road, on a snowy day, 15 December 1950. This building was built in 1848 as one of three lodges to the lord of the manor's game reserve on Worle Hill.

Gunnings Stores, Manchester Square, Worle, 28 May 1973. This was the oldest shop in the area. The building to the right was also part of the complex which included a granary, store, bakery, slaughterhouse and butcher's shop. It closed in 1985 and is now private housing.

The new Gateway Store, High Street, Worle, 7 June 1966. Some of the prices make interesting reading – cornflakes are 1s 10d. These were also the days when babies got to ride in proper coach-built prams.

New shops in the High Street, Worle, 25 May 1973. In 1970, Worle's population was expected to rise to twenty thousand over seven years. The High Street developments took place to cater for this increase.

The new branch library at Worle. This was built at the Maltings, and opened in 1969. A small estate of prefabricated bungalows was demolished to make way for this building and the flats also built at the same time. There were 10,000 books available when the library opened.

Capri Villas under construction, Toll Road, 1979. This is a terrace of split-level houses with spectacular sea views. Birnbeck Pier can be seen in the background.

Kewstoke village, 1956. This scene can hardly have changed since Victorian days, aside from the red telephone kiosk. Monks Hill, to the left, was still lit by gas lamps into the 1970s.

Filling Station and café, Beach Road, Sand Bay, 30 April 1960. These were the days when an attendant filled up your tank for you, took your money and returned with your change – what service!

Pontins Holiday Camp, Sand Bay, Kewstoke, 1960s. This is still a holiday camp today, although it was sold in September 2000 to Holly Bush Hotels and has been renamed. It specialises in adults-only breaks.

Uphill Way, Uphill, 1950s. One of the few views that has seen little change.

The new lounge at the Ship Hotel, Uphill, with Mr and Mrs Bye behind the bar, 2 May 1963. References to this building as a pub date back to at least 1782.